Dev[illegible]
Cook[illegible]ook

Margaret Wilson

Bossiney Books • Launceston

CONTENTS

Introduction 3
Starters 4
Savouries 9
Sweets 20
Cakes 27
Jams and pickles 31
Basic stocks and special pastries 35
Cider 39
Index of recipes 40

First published 1998 by
Bossiney Books, Langore, Launceston, Cornwall PL15 8LD

ISBN 1-899383-15-8

Cover photographs by Andrew Besley
Inside illustrations by Sara Silcock

Printed in Great Britain by R Booth Ltd, Mabe, Cornwall

INTRODUCTION

I was delighted to be asked to write about something that's been a huge part of my life for a long time now. Cooking for my family, friends and customers has always been a pleasure, a way for me to be inventive and to perfect my favourite recipes.

I trained at a well-known local hotel for eleven years before starting my own outside catering business. For many years my ambition has been to run my own restaurant. With the help and support of my husband, Paul, my dream came true on 13 July 1997 – our thirtieth wedding anniversary – when we turned our home into Tinhay Mill Restaurant. It is from here that all the Devonshire recipes for my book, some traditional, some new, have been tried and tested.

Devon is a feast of wonderful produce, with its beef farming and fishing, clotted cream and cider, Plymouth gin and lesser known Garland cheese. I've chosen recipes that reflect the variety of our local fresh ingredients to give you a taste of this beautiful county in your own home.

Before you rush off and try them for yourself, a few points to remember. Spoon measurements are always level, while eggs are size 2. Never mix imperial and metric measures. If you have an oven with a mind of its own, make adjustments to temperatures – mine are for guidance as much as anything. I mention parchment paper in a few of the recipes. It's better than greaseproof paper which tends to stick and, although it's quite expensive, you can save it and use it again. Muslin in the Restaurant kitchen is a must for straining stock, etc. It can be bought very cheaply in most fabric shops.

I do hope that my book will bring you as much pleasure and enjoyment as I have had in writing it.

Margaret Wilson, 1998

STARTERS

Leek and potato soup

(serves 6)

450 g (1 lb) potatoes, finely chopped
1 kg (2 lb 2 oz) leeks, finely chopped
125 g (4 oz) shredded leeks (blanched for
2 minutes in boiling water)
2 litres (3½ pints good chicken stock (see page 35))
2 tbsp clarified butter (see page 38)
seasoning
110 ml (4 fl oz) double cream
1 clove garlic, chopped

Place the chopped potatoes and a little salt in a large saucepan, and just cover them with cold water. Bring to the boil and blanch for 2 minutes. Strain the potatoes in a colander, setting aside the cooking liquid for later.

On a low heat, carefully melt the butter in a large saucepan and gently sauté the leeks with the chopped garlic until they are soft and without any colour. Add the potatoes and cook gently with the leeks for 5 minutes. Then add the chicken stock and continue to cook until the potatoes are soft. Place the soup in a blender and blast it until it is liquidised. You may need to do this twice, depending on the size of your blender. Add the potato liquid and the double cream. Check for seasoning. The soup is now ready to serve in warmed soup bowls. Decorate with a teaspoon of double cream and the finely shredded blanched leeks.

Layered fish loaf

(serves 6/8)

If you have kind fishmongers, ask them to fillet the fish for you and you'll make this dish in the blink of an eye.

2 large lemon sole, filleted/skinned
6 large trout fillets, skinned
2 tbsp Devonshire double cream
salt and cayenne pepper
1 egg, size 3
225 g (8 oz) half-fat cream cheese
125 g (5 oz) plain yoghurt
oil for greasing
1/4 tsp ground mace
75 g (3 oz) cooked spinach

Pre-heat the oven to 375°F /190°C /gas mark 5.

Start by oiling a 1 kg (2 lb) loaf tin and place the fish fillets between some damp greaseproof paper. Tap them very gently to flatten them a little. Place a layer of the sole at the bottom of your tin, then in your food processor mix the cheese, cream, yoghurt and egg. Next stir in the seasoning and the mace, and spoon a layer of this mixture over the fish, followed by a layer of cooked spinach and a layer of trout. Repeat this process until the tin is full, finishing with a layer of fish. Cover tightly with greaseproof paper and then a layer of tin foil. Place the tin in a roasting pan with 1 cm (1/2 inch) boiling water in the bottom.

Bake for 35-40 minutes or until the loaf feels firm. Leave it to cool in the tin and when it is completely cold put it into the fridge for 2 hours. Then the fun begins when you try to get it out of the tin! Have your oblong dish ready. Immerse the tin in a little boiling water for just 10 seconds to help free the loaf from the tin without getting any of the food warm. With a palette knife free the edges gently and turn out onto your serving dish.

Kipper pâté

350 g (12 oz) kipper flesh, with no bones attached
425 ml (3/4 pt) double cream
juice of 1 lemon
1/4 tsp mace
freshly ground black pepper
25 g (1 oz) clarified butter (see page 38)

The hardest part of this recipe is taking all those nasty little bones out of the kippers, but believe me the finished result is well worth the effort.

Put all the ingredients, except the cream, into the food processor and blend for 10 seconds. Then pulse in the cream carefully (every 2-3 seconds). Fill small ramekin pots with the finished pâté, cover with cling film and put into the fridge. Serve with freshly baked Devonshire splits (see page 27), a wedge of lemon and a side salad.

Country duck loaf

(serves 10 to 12 people)

If you are having a dinner party, this recipe makes a wonderful starter served with apple and apricot chutney with Devonshire cider (see page 34). Or if you are serving a buffet for a special occasion, it would be the perfect dish for elegance and taste. Arrange on an oblong dish with watercress, crispy salad leaves, nasturtiums and orange slices. (The recipe may appear to be a little fiddly, but if you follow the instructions carefully the end results are very rewarding.)

1 x 3 kg (6 lb) whole duckling (preferably free range)
375 g (12 oz) fatty smoked bacon, minced
375 g (12 oz) pork, coarsely minced
1 measure brandy
1 measure port

1 tbsp green peppercorns
1 tbsp crushed juniper berries
seasoning
1 egg
50 g (2 oz) butter
liver from the giblets

For the stock

1 litre (2 pints) cold water
75 ml (3 fl oz) vegetable oil
1 fresh bay leaf
1 sprig fresh thyme
1 clove garlic, crushed
1 carrot, peeled and chopped
1 medium-sized onion, chopped
1 white of leek, chopped
giblets, without the liver

You can take on the task of skinning the duck yourself, or you can ask your butcher to do it for you. If you do it yourself, you'll need a very sharp boning knife and a chopping board. Start by turning the duck upside down on the board so that its back is 'looking' at you. Make a cut from head to tail, and gradually ease the skin back from the flesh with your fingers and your small sharp knife. When you get to the legs and wings, the skin should pull off – like taking off a sweater! Take a 1 kg (2 lb) loaf tin and line it with the duck skin – skin side down, fat side up. Cover with greaseproof paper and refrigerate until later.

With the boning knife take the breast and cut it and the liver into thin strips. Place them in a basin with the port and brandy, and marinade for 2½ hours.

Then proceed to take the meat off the legs. On a shallow oven-proof dish put the carcass, leg bones, giblets (not the liver), carrot, onion, garlic and leeks. Cover with the vegetable oil and brown in the oven at 400°F/200°C/gas mark 6 for 30 minutes.

After this, put the water, bay leaf and thyme into a large saucepan, and add the browned ingredients from the oven. Simmer on the top of the stove for an hour. Then strain the liquid through fine muslin and put the stock back into the pan and simmer again until it has reduced to just 150 ml (5 fl oz). Have ready a bowl of ice cubes in which to immerse the stock vessel for it to cool as quickly as possible.

While the stock is cooking, mince the leg meat. Mix it in a large bowl with the bacon, pork, peppercorns, juniper, egg, 1/2 teaspoon of salt and 1 teaspoon of freshly milled black pepper. Take the liver and breast and strain the marinade into the meat. Then mix them together. Add the cooled stock and mix further until the liquid is well incorporated.

Next, melt the butter in a small pan and when it starts to bubble sauté the strips of duck breast and the liver for 2 minutes – just to seal in the juices. Place on a dish to drain. Then take your lined loaf tin from the fridge (don't forget to remove the greaseproof paper) and put a layer of the minced meat mix on the base.

Follow this with 3 strips of breast and 2 strips of the liver, and repeat, ending with a layer of meat mixture. Press down well, so it tucks into all the corners. Cover the top with the overlapping skin, and cover first with buttered greaseproof paper and then with tin foil.

Place on a tray, or you will end up with a nasty mess in your oven – the fat will bubble over! Put the tin on the middle shelf and cook at 350°F/180°C/gas mark 4 for 2 hours or until the loaf has shrunk from the side of the tin.

Take the loaf from the oven and allow it to cool. Put some weights on it and then refrigerate for at least 12 hours before turning it out onto the serving dish.

SAVOURIES

Devon leek or turnip pie

225 g (8 oz) Devon butter pastry (see page 38)
8 leeks
275 ml (1/2 pt) milk
salt and freshly milled pepper
110 ml (4 fl oz) single cream

Trim and wash the leeks and cut them into 2-3 cm (1 inch) pieces. Add them to the milk together with the seasoning, and simmer gently until tender. Stir in the cream and transfer to an oven-proof dish. Then cover with the rolled out pastry, egg wash and bake at 400°F/200°C/gas mark 6 for 25 minutes or until the pastry is cooked. To make turnip pie, use 450 g (1 lb) of turnips instead of the leeks and follow the recipe in the same way.

Pickled herrings

This recipe is so quick and easy to prepare, and is simply wonderful to eat, especially with fresh homemade bread.

6 herrings, filleted
2 shallots, thinly sliced
6 whole cloves
1 bay leaf
150 ml (1/4 pt) white wine vinegar
150 ml (1/4 pt) water
12 whole peppercorns
pinch of salt

Roll the herring fillets and place them in a baking dish. Add the sliced shallots and all the other ingredients. Bake at 350°F/180°C/gas mark 4 for 45 minutes to an hour. Leave to cool, cover with cling film and place in the fridge. They are now ready to eat.

Baked mackerel with apple, parsley and breadcrumb stuffing

(serves 4)

The freshest of mackerel should be used: look for bright, stiff fish rather than limp, tired ones.

4 mackerel, gutted and heads removed
75 g (3 oz) butter
100 g (4 oz) fresh white breadcrumbs
2 tbsp finely chopped fresh parsley
grated rind of 1 lemon
1 egg
2 shallots, finely chopped
100 g (4 oz) cooking apple (chopped and cover with half the lemon juice to stop the apple going brown)
salt and freshly milled black pepper
oil

Pre-heat the oven to 375°F/190°C/gas mark 5.

Start by washing and drying the mackerel thoroughly. Then, using a large frying pan, melt 50 g (2 oz) of the butter and gently cook the shallots (without colour) for about 2 minutes. In a mixing bowl place the breadcrumbs, parsley, lemon rind and apples, and add the egg to combine the mixture. Season well with the salt and freshly milled black pepper. The fish are now ready for stuffing.

Pack equal quantities into the stomach of each fish. Brush with the oil, put onto a baking tray and bake for 30 minutes. Then take the fish from the oven and melt the remaining butter in a small pan. When it starts to bubble, add the rest of the lemon juice and pour over the fish. Pop them back into the oven and bake for 3 minutes.

Serve with perhaps some freshly dug new potatoes cooked in their jackets and with parsley butter and a crisp salad.

Barbican fish cakes

(makes 6 large cakes or 12 small ones)

175 g (6 oz) cod, skinned and boned
175 g (6 oz) salmon, tail end (ask your fishmonger to skin and bone it for you)
2 tsp finely chopped fresh parsley
1 tsp chopped chives
2 tbsp béchamel sauce (see page 18)
350 g (12 oz) new potatoes (boil in their jackets for 10 minutes, leave to cool, peel and then coarsely grate them)
2 tbsp clarified butter (see page 38)
1/2 tsp sea salt
1/2 tsp freshly milled white pepper

Dice the fish into 2.5 cm (1 in) cubes and place them in a food processor. Pulse for 2-3 seconds or chop finely by hand if you haven't got a processor – sometimes I think it is just as quick, especially if you're using small quantities.

In a large mixing bowl put the chopped herbs, grated potato, béchamel sauce and the seasoning, and combine all the ingredients together. Divide into 6 or 12 cakes, depending on whether you want them as a starter or as a main course. Roll into balls, press down and make each into a round shape.

Heat the butter in a large sauté pan or frying pan and, when it starts to bubble, put the fish cakes in and cook for 3-4 minutes on either side or until golden brown. Drain on kitchen paper and serve.

Seared peppered Tamar salmon

(serves 6)

700 kg ($1^{1}/_{2}$ lb) fillet of Tamar salmon, with the skin on
2 tsp finely ground black pepper and 2 tsp salt
1 tsp caster sugar
1 tbsp olive oil and 2 tsp lime juice

With a pair of tweezers remove any little bones that may be left in the fish. Put the pepper through a sieve so that it is very fine and mix it with the salt, sugar, oil and lime juice. Coat the salmon with it, wrap in cling film and leave to marinade for 3 hours or more in the fridge.

Remove the cling film and cut into 6 portions. Put 1 tbsp oil in a small frying or sauté pan and when it is very hot put your salmon in, skinside down. It will take 20-25 seconds on either side. I serve this dish in my restaurant as a main course with a hot butter sauce. It also makes a very good starter.

For the butter sauce

75 g (3 oz) finely chopped shallots
200 g (7 oz) unsalted butter
3 tbsp white wine vinegar
75 ml (3 fl oz) water or fish stock (see page 36)
3 tbsp dry white wine and 3 tbsp double cream

Place the shallots, wine, vinegar and water or stock in a saucepan (a shallow pan is best, because the sauce doesn't take quite so long to make). Bring to the boil and cook until you have only 3 tablespoonsful left. Strain the liquid through a sieve, discarding the shallots. Put back into the saucepan onto the heat and add the double cream. Let it bubble for 30 seconds before adding the butter, a knob at a time. Whisk vigorously until all the butter is incorporated. The sauce is now ready to serve with your Tamar salmon.

Tavy trout with parsley and lemon butter

(serves 4)

4 whole trout (ask your fishmonger to clean them and take their heads off if you don't want to do it yourself)
freshly milled black pepper and sea salt
50 g (2 oz) clarified butter (see page 38)
2 tsp finely chopped fresh parley and 2 lemons

Brush the trout with half the butter, and season them. Place on a grilling tray under a very hot grill. Cook for 4 minutes on each side. While the trout are cooking, chop the parsley and mix it with the remaining butter and the juice of 1 lemon. Heat gently in a pan. When the fish is cooked and on warm plates, pour the lemon and parsley butter over. Garnish with parsley leaves and lemon wedges, and enjoy.

Leek and Devon garland stuffed jacket potatoes

4 x 225 g (8 oz) baking potatoes
350 g (12 oz) leeks, finely chopped
225 (8 oz) Devon Garland cheese, grated
clarified butter (see page 38)
110 ml (4 fl oz) Devonshire double cream
freshly milled pepper

Preheat the oven to 350°F /180°C /gas mark 4. Place the potatoes on a baking sheet and cook for 1 1/2 hours. While they are cooking, put 2 tablespoons of butter into a large saucepan and sauté the leeks for around 5 minutes until they are soft and without colour. Take off the heat, add the grated cheese and mix in the cream and pepper. Cut the cooked potatoes in half, scoop out the insides and mash them. Add the leek mixture and fill the cases. Put them back in the oven for 15-20 minutes or until they are golden brown. This recipe goes well with chicken.

Traditional roast rib of Devon beef with batter pudding

(serves 6)

1 x 2.25 kg (5 lb) rib of beef, boned and rolled
freshly milled black pepper
salt

When you buy your rib, look for a joint with a nice piece of fat around the outside. This will give it a really good flavour and it will taste more succulent. Pre-heat the oven to 425°F/220°C/gas mark 6.

Put your beef in a large roasting dish and season with salt and freshly milled pepper. Place the dish in the centre of the oven for 15 minutes to seal the meat, then turn the temperature down to 375°F/190°C/gas mark 5 and cook until your beef is as you prefer it.

For rare beef cook for 15 minutes per 450 g/1 lb. For medium rare add an extra 15 minutes at the end, and for well done, an extra 25 minutes.

During the cooking period take the meat out of the oven, tilt the pan and baste the beef with its own juices. When the joint is cooked, have a warm dish ready and transfer the meat onto it.

Leave it to 'relax' for 20 minutes, covered with foil, as this will allow time for the juices to be absorbed back into the joint before carving.

For the gravy
When straining the vegetables, keep the stock and use it for the gravy. You'll need about 1 litre (1 3/4 pints). You should also be left with some dripping and juices from the joint in your roasting tin. Tip out enough dripping for the batter into a basin, leaving any meat juice in the tin. Put this back onto the stove at medium heat. When it starts to bubble, add 2 tablespoons of plain flour, take the tin off the heat and add a little of your vegetable water, making a smooth paste. Then put the tin back on

the heat and whisk in the rest of the liquid gradually, making sure you have scraped all the juices from the bottom of the tin. Simmer for 2 minutes, which will reduce the liquid down and enhance the flavour. Check the seasoning, and serve.

For the batter pudding

I always use deep muffin tins for my batter puddings. This recipe makes 8. (You can always double the recipe if you want extra to eat as a pudding with warm maple syrup and Devonshire double cream!)

dripping from the beef
175 g (6 oz) plain flour, sifted
3 eggs
275 ml (10 fl oz) skimmed milk
freshly milled pepper
1/4 tsp salt

Divide the dripping between the tins and put into the pre-heated oven at 425°F/220°C/gas mark 7 until the fat is sizzling. Mix all the ingredients together – if you have an electric food processor, switch on for 1 minute.

Pour through a sieve into a jug. Carefully lift out the tins with the very hot fat and pour in equal quantities of the batter. Cook on the top shelf in the oven for 30-35 minutes. When cooked they should be golden brown and crispy.

Raised Devon pork pie

(serves 6)

For the filling

1.35 kg (3 lb) loin of pork, boned
350 g (12 oz) onions, finely chopped
350 g (12 oz) sliced dessert apples, sliced
275 ml (1/2 pt) dry Devon cider
2 tbsp sugar
salt and freshly milled black pepper
1/4 tsp each of all spice and freshly chopped sage
1/4 tsp freshly grated nutmeg

Wash, peel and chop the onions and slice the apple. Mince the pork into a large bowl and mix with all the other ingredients, including the cider.

For the hot water crust pastry

205 ml (7 fl oz) water
175 g (6 oz) lard
450 g (1 lb) plain flour and 1/2 tsp salt
1 egg

For this recipe you can buy a fancy tin especially for raised pies, but just as good is a loaf or cake tin (6 x 20 cm/2 1/2 x 8 in) depending on the shape you like. To make the pastry put the water and the lard in a saucepan and bring to the boil. While it is coming to the boil, sift the flour with the salt into a large bowl. Make a well in the centre, pour in the boiling liquid and stir very quickly until you have a smooth dough. Finally, add the egg, which will give the pastry its rich colour. Line whatever tin you choose to use. Fill it with your pork mixture, egg wash the edges, then cover with the remaining pastry. Trim the edge of the pie, using the cuttings to make some leaf shapes for decoration. Egg wash the top and bake the pie at 400°F/200°C/gas mark 6 for about 30 minutes or until the pie is a little golden. This helps firm up the pastry. Then lower the heat to 325°F/175°C/gas mark 3 for 1½ to 2 hours – you may have to cover the pie with foil to prevent it burning.

Devonshire beer and beef casserole with herby cobbler

(serves 6)

This is an excellent recipe for people who are too busy to spend much time preparing anything fiddly. It's a good winter warmer.

1.35 kg (3 lb) chuck steak, diced
3 large onions, finely chopped
350 g (12 oz) sliced carrots
350 g (12 oz) diced swede
2 tsp freshly chopped thyme
2 tsp freshly chopped parsley
½ tsp salt and 1 tsp freshly milled pepper
2 tbsp red lentils
1 fresh bay leaf
1 litre (1¾ pints) Devon beer
75 g (3 oz) plain flour
3 tbsp sunflower oil

First of all put the flour and seasoning into a large bowl. Take the diced meat and coat it with the flour. Then in a large pan heat the oil to a high temperature and brown and seal the meat instantly. Put the meat into a casserole dish with all the other ingredients, cover, and cook for 1 hour at 325°F/170°C/gas mark 3. Take the casserole out of the oven, give a good stir, cover and cook for a further 2 hours. Check for seasoning and liquid (you can always add more beer if need be), and arrange the herby scones on the top. Cook for 10-12 minutes at 400°F/200°C/gas mark 6. Serve on warmed plates with simple savoury basmati rice – delicious!

For the cobbler

225 g (8 oz) self-raising flour, sifted
50 g (2 oz) butter or margarine
1/4 tsp salt
150 ml (5 fl oz) milk
1/2 tsp finely chopped parsley
1/2 tsp finely chopped fresh thyme

In a mixing bowl rub the butter/margarine into the sifted flour. Add the salt and herbs, and gradually incorporate the milk until the mix forms a ball. You may need a little extra milk if the mix feels dry. Put the scone ball onto a lightly floured board and very gently roll out with a rolling pin to a thickness of 2 cm (3/4 in). Use a 5 cm (2 in) cutter and cut out your scones.

Béchamel sauce

This is a roux sauce made with infused milk.

425 ml (3/4 pt) milk
1 onion, sliced
1 stick celery, chopped
1 fresh bay leaf
6 whole peppercorns, crushed
1 carrot, chopped
parsley stalks
2 whole cloves
25 g (1 oz) butter
25 g (1 oz) plain flour

Place all the ingredients, except the butter and flour, in a saucepan and bring very gently to the boil. Remove from the heat and allow to infuse for 20 minutes.Then strain the liquid through a sieve into a jug and make the sauce as follows. Melt the butter in a saucepan, add the flour and cook for 2 minutes. (As this is for a white sauce, you must cook it without any colour, so have it on a very low heat.) This is the 'roux'. You are now ready for the infused milk: to prevent lumps, add a little at a time and thoroughly whisk each time until you have used all the liquid. Then cook gently for another 2 minutes.

Further ingredients can be added to this basic béchamel sauce.

Parsley sauce

3 tbsp chopped parsley
1 tsp lemon juice
1 tbsp single cream
15 g (1/2 oz) butter

Devon cheese sauce

50 g (2 oz) mature Devon cheddar cheese, grated
pinch of cayenne pepper
1 level tsp English mustard powder
150 ml (1/4 pt) single cream

Bread sauce

75 g (3 oz) white breadcrumbs (no crusts)
2 tbsp Devon double cream
15 g (1/2 oz) butter

Add the cream and the butter at the end for this sauce. It is then ready for serving.

SWEETS

Blackberry and apple cobbler

(serves 6)

This recipe is made with Devonshire apples and freshly picked blackberries, and is served with real Devonshire cream.

For the filling

1.35 kg (3 lb) cooking apples (washed, peeled, cored and sliced; cover with the juice of 1 lemon)
225 g (8 oz) fresh blackberries
40 g (1½ oz) butter
85 g (3½ oz) light soft brown sugar

For the scone mix

225 g (8 oz) sifted self-raising flour
50 g (2 oz) caster sugar
110 g (4 oz) Devonshire clotted cream
1 egg
150 ml (5 fl oz) milk to bind
2 tsp baking powder and pinch of salt

In a large saucepan melt the butter, add the apples and sugar, and cook gently for 10 minutes or until the apples are tender. Add the blackberries, place in an oven-proof dish and leave to cool. In the meantime, put the flour, baking powder, salt, sugar and cream in a mixing bowl. Gently break the cream into the flour. Then beat the egg and milk together and add to the flour. Gently mix together as lightly as possible. Leave to rest.

You will need a floured board and a 5 cm (2 in) cutter. Gently roll out the scone mix until it is 2 cm (¾ in) thick, and cut out the scones. Place on the top of the blackberry and apple. Bake in a pre-heated oven at 375°F / 190°C / gas mark 5 for 30 minutes or until the scone mix is cooked – if you gently touch a scone and it springs back, this usually means it's cooked!

Devonshire custard, with real Devon double cream

This vanilla custard goes very well with apple cake if you want to use it as a pudding. It is also delicious served cold.

8 egg yolks
110 g (4 oz) caster sugar and 1 vanilla pod
425 ml (12 fl oz) double cream
425 ml (12 fl oz full cream milk

Beat the egg yolks and the sugar in an electric mixer until you have a pale, thick and creamy mixture. Split the vanilla pod and scrape out the inside. Leave the seeds to infuse into the milk and cream while bringing them to the boil. Put a pan of simmering water on the heat and place the bowl of egg and sugar mixture over it. Stir in quickly the boiling milk and cream, and keep stirring until the mixture has thickened and coats the back of the spoon. Remove the custard from the heat and serve.

You now have 8 egg whites to use up, so why not try the recipe for Meringue roly poly on page 24. Egg whites (covered) will keep in the fridge for 2 or 3 days.

Devonshire junket

(serves 6)

570 ml (1 pt) full cream milk
1 tbsp sugar and 1 tbsp brandy
1 tsp rennet (vegetarian rennet is available if preferred)
freshly grated nutmeg
110 g (4 oz) Devonshire clotted cream

Warm the milk to blood temperature (98.4°F /37°C). Mix the brandy and the sugar in a bowl, then pour on the warmed milk. Add the rennet and place the junket in a cool area. When set, cover with freshly grated nutmeg, and serve with Devonshire clotted cream.

Devon cider sorbet

1 litre (2 pints) cold stock syrup (see page 36)
570 ml (1 pint) Devon cider

Mix all the stock syrup with all the cider and churn in an ice-cream maker for approximately 8 minutes. Then put the sorbet into a freezer-proof container and freeze.

If you are not lucky enough to own an ice-cream maker, it is a little harder but it doesn't really take too long. Start by placing a stainless steel bowl in the freezer to chill for 30 minutes before you make the sorbet.

Once made, put it into the bowl and freeze for an hour. Then take it out of the freezer and transfer it to your food processor. Blitz it for 30 seconds, put it back into the stainless steel bowl and freeze again. Repeat this process three times. Each time your sorbet should become more solid.

Plymouth gin and juniper sorbet

grated rind and juice of 2 lemons and 2 oranges
50 g (2 oz) juniper berries, crushed
570 ml (1 pt) stock syrup (see page 36)
110 ml (4 fl oz) Plymouth gin

Tie the crushed juniper berries into a square of muslin and let it simmer in the stock syrup for 3 minutes. Take off the heat and leave to infuse for 2 hours (or longer if you prefer). Then take out the muslin bag and discard it, but don't strain the liquid, as the citrus flavours from the lemon and orange in the stock syrup are just wonderful.

When cool, add the gin and churn for 8 minutes or freeze as for the Devon cider sorbet. Serve to your favourite friends whom you are sure to impress.

Midge Bruen's fudge pudding

This pudding is for the person with a very sweet tooth.

450 g (1 lb) small can golden syrup
2 tsp lemon juice
570 ml (1 pt) white sauce
roughly grated plain chocolate
serve with Devonshire double cream

Pour the syrup into a saucepan. (I find the easiest way to do this is to put the can – lid off – in a pan of water and bring it to the boil until the syrup is runny. This will enable you to get every scrap out of the can.) Boil slowly until it turns very brown in colour and caramelises. Don't let it overcook, or it will taste burnt. Add the lemon juice.

While the syrup is caramelising, make the white sauce.

For traditional white sauce (serves 6)

570 ml (1 pt) milk
50 g (2 oz) butter
40 g (1½ oz) plain flour

Melt the butter gently in a saucepan on a low heat – don't let the butter brown, as this will affect the flavour. Add the sifted plain flour and mix with a wooden spoon. Take off the heat and pour on the milk a little at a time, giving it a good stir each time to prevent lumps. If you don't rush, you should end up with a glossy lump-free sauce. However, if you're unfortunate enough to have a few lumps, you can correct it by using an electric whisk or by putting the sauce through a fine sieve. When all the milk has been mixed in, put the saucepan back on the lowest heat possible and cook for 5-8 minutes to thicken.

Mix the hot white sauce with the caramelised syrup, place in ramekins and leave to cool. When cold, cover each with a tablespoon of the roughly grated chocolate and serve with cream.

Meringue roly poly with Midge Bruen's fudge filling

If you have some egg whites to use up, meringue seems to be almost everyone's favourite. But choice of filling can be difficult. I actually made this recipe for a dinner party for Bernie (son of Midge) and it was a great hit for them. It serves 10-12, but you could always make two meringues and freeze one – wrapped in foil they freeze well, though do remember they take up to 6 hours to thaw.

For the meringue

8 egg whites
450 g (1 lb) caster sugar
75 g (3 oz) crushed pecan nuts

For the filling

Midge Bruen's fudge pudding (see page 23), cool but not cold
600 ml (6 oz) double cream
175 g (6 oz) roughly grated good quality plain chocolate

You will need a Swiss roll tin (33 x 23 cm/13 x 9 in) and a sheet of parchment paper to line it. Start by pre-heating the oven to 375°F/190°C/gas mark 5.

Line the tin with parchment. Whisk the egg whites in a mixer at full speed until they are very stiff. Slow the mixer down to half speed and add the sugar a tablespoon at a time, leaving 5 seconds between each spoonful to mix thoroughly.

Spread the meringue evenly in the tin, sprinkle with the nuts over the top and put in the centre of the oven. Bake for 10-15 minutes or until it is lightly browned. Turn the oven down to 300°F/150°C/gas mark 2 and bake for a further 20 minutes.

Prepare a sheet of parchment paper on the table 10 cm (4 in) wider than the Swiss roll tin. Turn the roly poly out, nut side down, onto the paper and leave for 8 minutes to cool. While it's cooling, whip the double cream – make sure it's not too stiff, or it will be hard to spread. Remove the paper from the base of the meringue. Then put a layer of cream all over the meringue, and follow this with a layer of chocolate and finally the fudge pudding.

Next take a deep breath, close your eyes and pray! Take the longest side and start to roll, keeping it as tight as possible. You should be able to roll it along with the parchment paper very gently – the paper helps to stop it breaking too much. Refrigerate until you are ready to serve.

Rice pudding with Plymouth gin

This pudding takes 4 hours to cook on a very low heat.

60 g (2½ oz) pudding rice
1.2 litres (2 pints) single cream
2 tbsp caster sugar
25 g (1 oz) butter
75 ml (3 fl oz) Plymouth gin
freshly grated nutmeg

Put the rice in an oven-proof dish with half the sugar and cream, and the butter and gin. Bake in the oven on a low heat (275°F/140°C/gas mark 1). After 2 hours give the pudding a good stir, and add the rest of the cream and sugar, together with the freshly grated nutmeg.

Cook for a further 2 hours, reducing the heat to 225°F/120°C/gas mark ½.

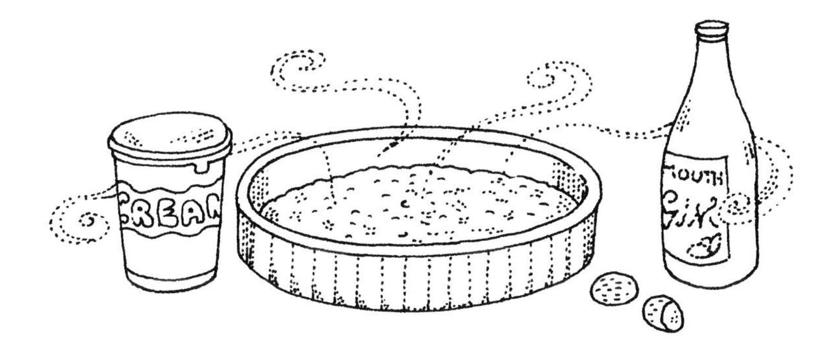

Goosey Fair toffee apples

(makes 8)

Goosey Fair comes to Tavistock on the second Wednesday in October every year.

8 dessert apples
350 g (12 oz) demerara sugar
75 g (3 oz) unsalted butter
4 tbsp vinegar

8 x 13 cm (5 in) wooden sticks
1 small bowl of cold water

Begin by washing the apples. Completely dry them with kitchen paper and push them onto the wooden sticks.

Next take a heavy-bottomed saucepan and into it put the sugar and butter. Place it on a low heat until the sugar has dissolved, and add the vinegar. Boil the mixture rapidly – it will become dark brown in colour.

To test the toffee, drop a small amount into the little bowl with cold water. If it becomes brittle, this means it is ready and you can now swirl the apples in the mixture until they are completely coated.

Have a baking sheet ready to place them on while they set and leave them until they are completely cold. The kids will love them!

CAKES

Devonshire splits

Devonshire splits are delicious served hot with butter or cold with homemade strawberry jam (see page 32) and Devonshire clotted cream.

450 g (1 lb) plain flour
1/2 tsp salt
10 g (1/2 oz) fresh yeast
1 tsp caster sugar
25 g (1 oz) butter
275 ml (1/2 pt) skimmed milk

When making yeast goodies, I always warm the bowl and the sifted flour first, as this helps to speed things up – yeast cooking can be a long process. Just pop the bowl in the oven for 10 seconds to take the chill off.

Add the salt to the warm flour. Warm the milk to blood temperature (98.4°F/37°C) and cream the yeast with a little of it in a separate bowl. Melt the butter in the remaining warm milk. Make a well in the centre of the flour and pour in the milk, butter and yeast. Mix and knead into a dough.

Cover the mixture with cling film and a clean tea towel, and leave to prove for 45 minutes to 1 hour (or when it is double in size). Break the dough into 12 little balls and knead each into shape on a warm greased oven tray.

Leave to prove for a further 15-20 minutes. Brush them with milk and a generous sprinkling of flour. Bake for 15-20 minutes at 375°F/190°-200°C/gas mark 5-6.

Devonshire apple cake

225 g (8 oz) plain flour
1 tsp bicarbonate of soda
$^1/_2$ tsp cinnamon
$^1/_2$ tsp ground ginger
$^1/_2$ tsp mixed spice
275 g (10 oz) mixed dried fruit
2 eggs
450 g (1 lb) cooking apples, peeled and sliced
150 g (5 oz) Devonshire butter
175 gm (6 oz) soft brown sugar
pinch of salt
caster sugar for dredging
grated rind of 1 lemon
2 tbsp Devon cider

Line a 20 cm (8-inch) shallow cake tin with parchment paper. Prepare the apples and cook them in the cider until they are soft. Liquidise them and measure out 225 ml (8 fl oz) of the sauce.

Cream together the butter, sugar and lemon rind, and then beat the eggs in, one at a time. Sieve in the dry ingredients (flour, spices and bicarbonate of soda), and fold in alternately the flour, etc, the fruit and the cold apple purée.

When everything is well incorporated, place the mixture into the prepared cake tin and dredge it with caster sugar.

Bake in the centre of the oven at 325°F/170°C/gas mark 3 for 1 to $1^1/_2$ hours.

Devonshire saffron cake

3/4 tsp saffron strands (soak in 55ml (2 fl oz)
hot water over night)
1 kg (2 lb 2 oz) plain flour
25 g (1 oz) fresh yeast
1/4 tsp mixed spice
1/4 tsp salt
225 g (8 oz) caster sugar
110 g (4 oz) butter
110 g (4 oz) lard
50 g (2 oz) candied lemon and orange peel
350 g (12 oz) mixed dried fruit
275 ml (1/2 pt) warmed milk
75 ml (3 fl oz) warm water

Mix together 1 tsp sugar, the warm water and 2 tbsp flour. Add the yeast and leave to rise in a warm place for 25 minutes.

In the meantime sieve the flour into a large warmed mixing bowl and rub in the butter and the lard until the mixture resembles fine bread crumbs. Add the salt, spices and sugar, and then the yeast mixture together with the luke warm milk, soaked saffron and the dried fruit. Mix well for 2 minutes.

Cover with a clean cloth and leave in a warm place for approximately 1 hour or until it is double in size.

Grease two 900 g/2 lb loaf tins and divide the mixture between them. Leave to prove again, this time for 20 minutes, and then bake for 40-45 minutes at 425°F/220°C/gas mark 7.

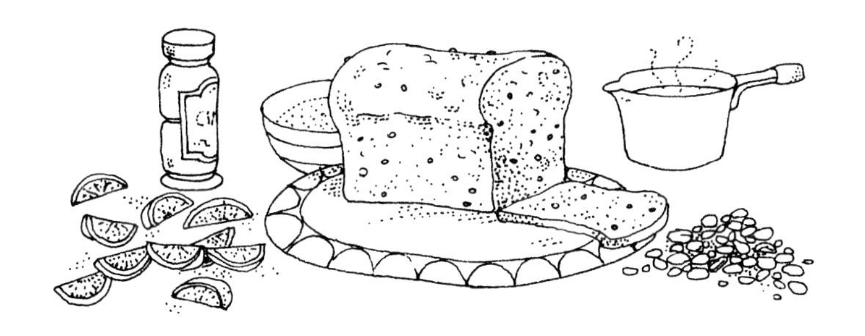

Devonshire flats

(makes about 36 flats)

225 g (8 oz) Devonshire clotted cream
450 g (1 lb) plain flour
1 egg
225 g (8 oz) caster sugar
milk

Rub the cream into the flour. Then beat in the egg and a little milk, and add the sugar. Mix to a smooth dough, and roll out very thinly. Cut into 7-8 cm (3-inch) rounds and sprinkle them with a touch of sugar. Bake at 375°F/190°C/gas mark 5 for 10 minutes.

Orchard cake

225 g (8 oz) self-raising flour
1 tsp baking powder
1/4 tsp mixed spice
25 g (1 oz) currants
1 egg
1 small (150 ml/5 fl oz) can evaporated milk
225 g (8 oz) sliced, uncooked cooking apples
100 g (4 oz) Devon butter: reserve 25 g (1 oz)
125 g (5 oz) brown sugar: reserve 50 g (2 oz)
pinch of salt

Line a loaf tin measuring 23 x 11 x 6 cm (9 x 4 1/2 x 2 1/2 in) with parchment paper. Rub together the sieved flour, baking powder, spice and salt, and 75 g (3 oz) each of the butter and sugar. Add the milk, egg and currants. When everything is well mixed in, place into the prepared tin and then arrange the sliced apples on top. Spread the remaining butter and reserved sugar over them. Bake for 1 hour at 350°F/180°C/gas mark 4. This cake is delicious served hot or cold.

JAMS AND PICKLES

When preserving or pickling, you will inevitably need lots of jars. You can buy special preserving jars with lids that seal properly, but they are quite expensive and unnecessary if you save all the jars that come your way – sizes aren't that important. To sterilise them, you should wash them thoroughly first in hot soapy water. Then rinse in clear hot water with 1 Milton tablet (used for sterilising baby bottles) and leave for 5 minutes. Dry thoroughly with a clean tea towel and put into a moderate oven to keep them warm and, importantly, to prevent them from shattering when you fill them with your preserve.

When testing to see if your jam will set, have a cold saucer ready. Put one tablespoon onto the saucer and leave to cool for a few seconds. Then push the jam away from you with your finger. If it wrinkles, it is ready. If it hasn't set, you'll need to boil it for a further 5 minutes and repeat the saucer trick until it will do so.

Aunty Ellen's marrow jam

(makes approximately 3 kg/7 lb)

1 x 2 kg (4 1/4 lb) marrow, diced (skin taken off, seeds taken out)
2 tsp ground ginger
875 ml (25 fl oz) medium sweet cider
2.25 kg (5 lb) granulated sugar

In a large bowl place the prepared marrow, ginger and sugar. Cover it with a clean cloth and leave overnight in a cool place. Next day transfer the marrow into a large preserving pan, and add the cider. On a low heat bring everything to the boil, then simmer for 40 minutes or until the jam is cooked – when cooked the marrow should be slightly transparent and still quite chunky. Pour the jam into warm sterilised jars while still hot, and seal.

If you have never made marrow jam before, I can guarantee that once you have followed this recipe there will be no stopping you. For one thing, it is so easy, and for another, it is very cheap to make. Try it with freshly made scones and Devonshire clotted cream.

Strawberry jam

I make only small amounts of jam at any one time, as I find it sets much better and has much more flavour. You also get a richer colour. You can leave the strawberries whole or you can slice them. Either way, the jam is delicious – I use local strawberries from Lifton. This recipe makes 1.35 kg (3 lb).

1 kg (2 lb 2 oz) fresh strawberries
1 kg (2 lb 2 oz) sugar

Layer the strawberries, either whole or sliced, in a bowl. Sprinkle each layer with sugar, then cover and leave overnight. The first job next morning is to put everything into a preserving pan or a good heavy-bottomed saucepan. Bring to the boil and keep on a high heat for 7 minutes. Make sure you don't turn your back on the jam, as it could boil over or burn. If you think it is going to do either of these things, turn the heat down slightly.

Turn to simmering point and continue cooking for a further 20 minutes.

To test if the jam is at setting stage, take a cold saucer and pour out 1 tablespoon of the jam and leave it to cool. If it wrinkles, then it is ready.

If it doesn't, then you need to simmer for a further 5 minutes and test again. Pour the jam into pre-warmed sterilised jars and leave it to settle for 5 minutes before covering and sealing.

You can buy good jam funnels quite cheaply these days from most cook shops. They don't make as much mess as trying to use a spoon, so they're a worthwhile investment.

Devonshire apple and cucumber pickle

This recipe complements a number of cold meats and smoked local salmon, or is delicious with seared peppered Tamar salmon (see page 12).

2 kg (4 lb) cucumber, peeled and sliced thinly
1 kg (2 lb) Devonshire cooking apples, peeled and finely chopped
450 g (1 lb) shallots, peeled and finely chopped
2 green chillies, de-seeded and finely chopped
600 ml (1 pt) white wine vinegar
225 g (8 oz) muscavado sugar
25 g (1 oz) salt
2 tsp whole grain mustard
1 tsp ground turmeric and 1 tsp freshly grated ginger
1 tsp freshly grated nutmeg and 2 tbsp lemon juice

Prepare the cucumbers and sprinkle them with the salt. Leave them to drain for 1½ hours in a covered colander with a heavy weight on top. While they are draining, chop the shallots and chillies, and then peel, core and chop the apples finely. Cover them with the lemon juice to stop them going brown.

In a large pan put together all the spices, vinegar, apples and sugar, and bring them to the boil. Stir with a wooden spoon until all the sugar has dissolved and then continue cooking for a further 2 minutes. Add the cucumbers, shallots and chillies, bring back to the boil for 2 more minutes, and then put the pickle into clean sterilised jars. (When handling chillies avoid touching your eyes, as they will make them burn! They can also burn your hands, so you may prefer to wear some very thin rubber gloves.) Cover and seal while the mixture is hot. Store in a cool dark place for three weeks. If you're anything like me, you won't be able to wait that long – it's just so good. The Devonshire apples give the taste that little extra edge.

Apple and apricot chutney with Devonshire cider

(makes approximately 1.35 kg/3 lb)

450 g (1 lb) dried apricots (good quality)
375 g (12 oz) brown muscavado sugar
1.5 litres ($2\frac{1}{2}$ pints) white wine vinegar
250 ml ($\frac{1}{2}$ pint) cider
225 g (8 oz) cooking apples, chopped
3 red chillies, chopped very small
3 large onions, chopped
2 level tsp salt
2 tsp mustard seeds
3 level tsp ground ginger
3 level tsp ground coriander

I serve this chutney in my restaurant with Country duck loaf (see page 6), and it is very popular. If you don't like your chutney too hot, then I suggest you leave out the chillies.

Using a preserving pan or a large saucepan, soak the apricots in the vinegar and cider (with the sugar added) overnight.

Next day add all the other ingredients and put the pan on the stove to simmer, giving a good stir occasionally. Leave to simmer gently for approximately $1\frac{1}{2}$ hours.

You'll notice that the apricots soak up the liquid, so don't turn your back for long periods – you must stir every 5 minutes towards the end and watch out for sticking: after all this effort you don't want a burnt pan and no chutney! Leave the pan to stand for 30 minutes, then put your chutney into your warm sterilised jars and seal them. Store in a dry cool place.

BASIC STOCKS AND SPECIAL PASTRIES

Chicken stock

(makes 2.25 litres/4 pints)

1.35 kg (3 1/2 lb) chicken carcasses, chopped
110 g (4 oz) chicken livers
2 large onions, roughly chopped
2 large carrots, roughly chopped
2 leeks, chopped
2 stalks of celery, chopped
parsley stalks
12 whole peppercorns
1 crushed clove of garlic
3.4 litres (6 pints) water
1 sprig fresh thyme
1 bay leaf
50 g (2 oz) butter

Melt the butter in a large pan and sweat off the vegetables until they are soft. Add the chicken carcasses and liver, fresh herbs, peppercorns, crushed garlic and water, and bring to the boil (leaving the lid off).

Skim the surface to remove the scum, and turn down the heat and simmer for 2 hours. Then strain the stock through a sieve and leave it to cool. Skim off any fat with a spoon and strain again through some fine muslin.

To cool your stock quickly, have a bowl of ice cubes ready and immerse your pot of stock into it. As soon as it is cool, cover and refrigerate. You can freeze your stock in small quantities and use as required.

Fish stock

(makes 1.2 litres/ 2 pints)

1 large onion, sliced
1 stick celery, chopped
1 fresh bay leaf
6 whole peppercorns, crushed
675 g (1½ lb) white fish bones
parsley stalks
1 carrot and 1 leek, chopped
pinch of salt
1 litre (1¾ pints) water
275 ml (½ pint) white wine or dry cider

Put everything into a large saucepan, bring it to the boil and simmer for 20 minutes. Allow it to cool, then strain the stock through fine muslin.

Stock syrup

I use stock syrup all the time for my sorbets, poaching fresh fruit and making jellies and fresh fruit salad. If you're having a children's party you can make great ice lollies. Or for a cocktail party, why not try some liqueur ice?

This simple recipe makes 1 litre (2 pints). It will keep for ever, as long as it is in the fridge, but because it is so easy to make you may as well do it when you need it or perhaps the day before.

1 kg (2 lb 2 oz) sugar
1 l (2 pts) cold water
rind and juice of 2 lemons and 2 oranges

Place all the ingredients into a saucepan and gently bring to the boil. Once it is boiling, turn down the heat and simmer, stirring all the time until the sugar has dissolved. Then take the pan off the heat and leave it to cool. Once it is cool, put the liquid into a covered vessel and pop it into the fridge until you are ready to use it. If you want to cool it down quickly, have some ice cubes ready in a large bowl and put your pan of stock syrup into it.

Rose crust pastry

For any dessert cooking that needs a melt in the mouth sweet pastry, this one is the best by far. I've tasted a lot of sweet pastry in my time, and it is either hard or soggy. Rose crust knocks the lot for six. I was given the recipe by a friend years ago and I use it often – it's a must for mince pies at Christmas, is very easy to make and you can also freeze it.

175 g (6 oz) plain flour, sifted
150 g (5 oz) soft margarine
50 g (2 oz) corn flour
50 g (2 oz) icing sugar, sifted

Ideally, you need a food processor. Place all the ingredients in together and blend for 10 seconds. Everything should be well mixed together and should have formed a soft ball. Take this out, wrap it in cling film and refrigerate for 30 minutes.

Roll the pastry out on a floured surface. Line each pie tin with parchment circles – as the pastry is very crumbly, you must take this precaution to help you lift it out. Cut out pastry circles to the size you need and line the tins.

Fill your cases with the filling of your choice (e.g. mincemeat, apple purée, apricot, gooseberry, cherry), cut out the lids, and cover bake in a pre-heated oven at 325°F/170°C/gas mark 3 for 25 to 30 minutes. The pastry will feel firm and will just be beginning to turn a very pale golden colour when cooked.

When you take your pies out of the oven, leave them to cool in the tins for 5 minutes. Remove them carefully with a knife and put them on a cooling rack. Dredge them with icing sugar and serve with plenty of Devonshire double or clotted cream.

Devon butter pastry

This is another delicious pastry, and I have to admit to making Cornish pasties with it! You can use it for both savoury and sweet baking.

350 g (12 oz) plain flour, sifted
200 g (8 oz) Devonshire butter, chopped
4 tbsp very cold water

Put the flour and butter into a food processor and blend for 5 seconds or until the mixture resembles fine breadcrumbs. Then pulse in the cold water until a ball is formed.

You may need a little extra water, but only add a few drops at a time. Refrigerate for 30 minutes and then use as required. This pastry should be cooked at 400°F /200°C /gas mark 6.

Clarified butter

225 g (8 oz) unsalted butter

Clarified butter is the oily part of butter without the buttermilk. Place the butter in a pan over a low heat until it has melted and is just beginning to bubble. Add 1/2 teaspoon of cold water and take it off the heat. Allow it to cool, by which time it will have separated, leaving the oily butter on top.

Skim off the oil, leaving the solids and water to be thrown away. If you have a microwave there is a much easier method. Place the butter in a microwave proof bowl, cover with cling film and set your microwave on high for 1 minute. When you take the bowl out, the butter should have melted and separated out.

Clarified butter tends not to burn and also gives a good flavour to your cooking. If you want first-class results, then this is well worth the effort.

CIDER

Devonshire cider

(makes 9 litres/2 gallons)

3.5 kg (8 lb) cooking apples
9 litres (2 gallons) boiling water
25 g (1 oz) root ginger
3 lemons, squeezed
3.5 kg (8 lb) granulated sugar
150 ml (1/4 pt) boiling water

A large plastic dustbin with a lid is ideal for making cider. Don't use anything that's metal unless it's stainless steel.

Roughly cut the apples (just washed and nothing removed) and cover them with the boiling water. Leave them for 2 weeks, but from time to time crush and press them.

Then strain them and add the lemon juice, root ginger and sugar to the liquid. Add the 1/4 pint of boiling water and leave to stand for another 2 weeks. Remove the scum as it rises to the top.

At the end of the fortnight, strain through fine muslin into screw-top bottles. Lightly screw down for 2 days, then tighten the stoppers and keep in a cool place for 2 months after which the cider is ready to drink.

INDEX OF RECIPES

apple
  apple and apricot chutney 34
  apple and cucumber pickle 33
  apple cake 28
  apple stuffing 10
apples, toffee 26

blackberry and apple cobbler 20
batter pudding 14
béchamel sauce 18
beef, casserole with beer 17
  roast rib 14
bread sauce 19
butter, clarified 38
  parsley and lemon 13
  pastry 38

cakes 27-30
cheese sauce 19
chicken stock 35
chutney, apple and apricot 34
cider 39
  sorbet 22
cobbler, blackberry and apple 20
custard, Devonshire 21

duck, country loaf 6

fish
  cakes 11
  loaf 5
  stock 36
flats, Devonshire 30
fudge pudding, Midge Bruen's 23

gin, Plymouth, and juniper sorbet 22

herrings, pickled 9

jam, Aunty Ellen's marrow 31
  strawberry 32
junket, Devonshire 21

kipper pâté 6

leek pie 9
leek and potato soup 4
lemon and parsley butter 13

mackerel, baked 10
meringue roly poly 24

orchard cake 30

parsley sauce 19
pastries 37-38
pâté, kipper 6
pickle, Devonshire apple and
  cucumber 33
pork pie, raised Devon 16
potatoes, leek and Devon garland 13

rice pudding with Plymouth gin 25
rose crust pastry 37

saffron cake 29
salmon, seared peppered 12
sauces 18-19
savouries 9-19
soup, leek and potato 4
sorbet, cider 22
  Plymouth gin and juniper 22
splits, Devonshire 27
starters 4-8
stocks 35-37
stuffing
  apple, parsley and breadcrumb 10
syrup stock 36
sweets 20-26

toffee apples, Goosey Fair 26
trout, Tavy 13
turnip pie 9